WHEN I LOSE MY TEMPER

by Michael Gordon

THIS BOOK BELONGS TO

....

....

AGE: ....

While Josh was getting ready for a trip to the park,
Outside the window, the sky became cloudy and dark.

Rain pelted down and Mom said, "We'll have to wait to go out."

This made Josh mad. He huffed and stomped and started to shout.

He was hot and bothered and his anger started to swell.

He wanted to make it go away; it made him feel unwell.

"I'll teach you to calm down," said Mom. "You'll feel better soon.

Breathe in deeply until your tummy looks like a balloon."

"Then hold it, count to four, and breathe out all of the bad."
Josh repeated this technique until he stopped feeling mad.
"The rain won't last, Josh. We'll go to the park later and play.
Sometimes things don't go as planned, but that shouldn't ruin our day."

EXHALE

INHALE

EXHALE

INHALE

When it was time to turn off the TV and get ready for bed,
Josh said, "I don't want to. I want to watch my cartoons instead."
He grew angry again — and squeezed his little fists tight.
He felt like screaming and kicking — he didn't feel all right.

He struggled to control it because anger made him feel sad.

He tried Mom's balloon breathing, but he still felt so bad.

Dad said, "Let's add to Mom's technique. Dragon breaths are good.

We'll make our balloon bellies, then roar like a fierce dragon would."

Dad breathed in with Josh, then they both counted to four.

Then they let out their breath with a loud dragon roar.

Before long, Josh and Dad were laughing and having so much fun.
Josh ran off to give Mom a big hug and tell her what he'd done.

Later in the week, Emma had friends come over for the day.

Josh thought his sister's friends were fun and he wanted to play.

But Emma said Josh was too little when he asked to join in.

When his sister said "No," Josh got angry all over again.

His breaths became shorter — he got a pain in his head.

Then his breathing got faster and his face became red.

He remembered to breath in slowly and hold it for four.

Then he exhaled his breath with a fierce dragon roar.

The girls got a bit scared and Josh still didn't feel good.

He wondered why it wasn't working as well as it should.

So, he tried breathing deeper while counting to ten.

Then he exhaled his dragon fire and did it over again.

His plan started working — he felt less angry inside.

Fixing the problem by himself filled Josh full of pride.

Emma's friends went home and Josh's came over later that day,
He felt so happy that he invited Emma to play.

The End

HOW ANGER FEELS!

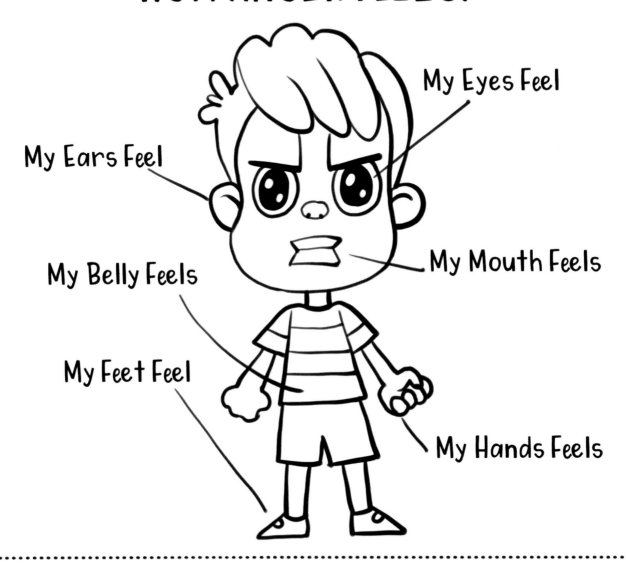

My Eyes Feel

My Ears Feel

My Mouth Feels

My Belly Feels

My Feet Feel

My Hands Feels

When I Lose My Temper, I will...

_____   _____   _____

Michael Gordon is the talented author of several highly rated children's books including the popular Sleep Tight, Little Monster, and the Animal Bedtime.

He collaborates with the renowned Kids Book Book that creates picture books for all of ages to enjoy. Michael's goal is to create books that are engaging, funny, and inspirational for children of all ages and their parents.

Contact

For all other questions about books or author, please e-mail michaelgordonclub@gmail.com.

Go https://michaelgordonclub.wixsite.com/books
to get "The Grumpy Dinosaur"
for **FREE!**